Dr Helen Kennerley qualified in Clinical Psychology in Oxford, where she also trained to become a cognitive therapist. She is one of the founder members of the Oxford Cognitive Therapy Centre (OCTC). Currently, she works as a consultant within OCTC, where she is the lead clinician of a specialist clinic in cognitive therapy. Helen has presented many workshops pertaining to her areas of clinical expertise both nationally and internationally. In 2002 she was shortlisted by the British Association for Behavioural and Cognitive Psychotherapies for the award for most influential female cognitive therapist in Britain.

The Overcoming series was initiated by Peter Cooper, Professor of Psychology at the University of Reading and Honorary NHS Consultant Clinical Psychologist. His original book on bulimia nervosa and binge-eating founded the series in 1993 and continues to help many thousands of people in the USA, the UK and Europe. The aim of the series is to help people with a wide range of common problems and disorders to take control of their own recovery programme using the latest techniques of cognitive behavioural therapy. Each book, with its specially tailored programme, is devised by a practising clinician. Many books in the Overcoming series are now recommended by the UK Department of Health under the Books on Prescription scheme.

Other titles in the Overcoming series:

3-part self-help courses

Overcoming Low Self-Esteem Self-Help Course
Overcoming Bulimia Nervosa and Binge-Eating Self-Help Course

Single volume books

Overcoming Anger and Irritability
Overcoming Anorexia Nervosa
Overcoming Anxiety
Bulimia Nervosa and Binge-Eating
Overcoming Childhood Trauma
Overcoming Chronic Fatigue
Overcoming Chronic Pain
Overcoming Compulsive Gambling
Overcoming Depression
Overcoming Insomnia and Sleep Problems
Overcoming Low Self-Esteem
Overcoming Mood Swings
Overcoming Obsessive Compulsive Disorder
Overcoming Panic
Overcoming Relationship Problems
Overcoming Sexual Problems
Overcoming Social Anxiety and Shyness
Overcoming Traumatic Stress
Overcoming Weight Problems
Overcoming Your Smoking Habit

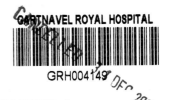
OVERCOMING ANXIETY
SELF-HELP PROGRAMME

A 3-part programme based on
Cognitive Behavioural Techniques

Part One: Understanding Anxiety

Helen Kennerley

ROBINSON
London

Constable & Robinson Ltd
3 The Lanchesters
162 Fulham Palace Road
London W6 9ER
www.overcoming.co.uk

First published in the UK by Robinson,
an imprint of Constable & Robinson Ltd 2006

A copy of the British Library Cataloguing in
Publication Data is available from the British Library.

Important Note
This book is not intended as a substitute for medical advice or treatment.
Any person with a condition requiring medical attention should consult
a qualified medical practitioner or suitable therapist.

ISBN 13: 978-1-84529-235-5 (Pack ISBN)
ISBN 10: 1-84529-235-9

ISBN 13: 978-1-84529-416-8 (Part One)
ISBN 10: 1-84529-416-5

ISBN 13: 978-1-84529-417-5 (Part Two)
ISBN 10: 1-84529-417-3

ISBN 13: 978-1-84529-418-2 (Part Three)
ISBN 10: 1-84529-418-1

1 3 5 7 9 10 8 6 4 2

Printed and bound in the EU

Contents

Contents

Foreword

The *Overcoming Anxiety Self-Help Course* is an adaptation of Dr Helen Kennerley's *Overcoming Anxiety* self-help book. This book provided a clear account of the nature of anxiety and its development, and a set of strategies for tackling the various components of the problem. These strategies derive from what is known as a 'cognitive-behavioural' formulation of the problem – that is, they are strategies designed to change the behaviour and thoughts associated with anxiety. The book, first published in 1997, has helped several thousand people in Britain and elsewhere with anxiety problems and it continues to prove enormously popular. It is regarded with considerable respect within the UK clinical community and is widely recommended. In this new form, as a set of workbooks, it has been updated and reformatted to make it even more accessible and easy to use.

In Part One of the workbooks, Dr Kennerley explains what anxiety is and how it could be affecting you, as well as how it develops. In Part Two, she examines ways of dealing with the symptoms of anxiety. Finally, in Part Three, Dr Kennerley offers guidance on how to cope with anxiety in the long run, as well as advice on time management, assertiveness and sleep.

Professor Peter Cooper
University of Reading, December 2005

Note to Practitioners

This self-help course is suitable for a wide range of reading abilities and its step-by-step format makes it ideal for working through alone or under supervision. The course is divided into three workbooks, and each contains a full supply of worksheets and charts to be filled in on the page – so there is no need for photocopying. If you do decide to photocopy this material you will need to seek the permission of the publishers to avoid a breach of copyright law.

Introduction: How to Use this Workbook

This is a self-help course for dealing with problem worries, fears and anxieties. It has two aims:

1 To help you develop a better understanding of the problem

2 To teach you some practical coping skills

How the course works

The *Overcoming Anxiety Self-Help Course* will help you understand how anxiety develops and what keeps it going, and then to make changes in your life so that you begin to feel more confident.

These workbooks are designed to help you work, either by yourself or with your healthcare practitioner, to overcome anxiety. With plenty of questionnaires, charts, worksheets and practical exercises, the three parts together make up a structured course.

Part One explains the origins and development of problem worries, fears and anxieties. You will learn:

- What anxiety and stress are
- Whether you have a problem with anxiety
- What the difference is between helpful short-term anxiety and unhelpful long-term anxiety
- Why anxiety has become a problem for you
- The cycles that maintain and worsen your anxiety
- What kind of anxiety disorder you might be suffering from

Part Two explains:

- How to ease the physical sensations of anxiety through controlled breathing and relaxation techniques

- How to deal with worrying thoughts

- How to face your fears using planning and problem-solving

Part Three gives advice on:

- Assertiveness training to help you handle relationships better

- Time management to help you improve decision-making and your organizational skills

- Sleep management to help you get a better night's rest

- Guidance for coping with anxiety in the long term

How long will the course take?

Although it will vary from person to person, it will probably take you at least two or three weeks to work through each workbook. You should not worry if you feel that you need to give certain parts extra time. Some things can be understood or practised quite quickly, but others may take longer. You will know when you are ready to move on to the next workbook. Completing the entire course could take two to three months, or it could take more or less time – it depends how quickly you wish to work.

Getting the most from the course

Here are some tips to help you get the most from the workbooks:

- These workbooks are not priceless antiques – they are practical tools. So feel free not only to write on the worksheets and charts, but also to underline and highlight things, and to write comments and questions in the margins. By the time you have finished with a workbook, it should look well and truly used.

- You will also find lots of space in the main text. These are for you to write down your thoughts and ideas, and your responses to the questions.

- Keep an open mind and be willing to experiment with new ideas and skills. These books will sometimes ask you to think about painful issues. However, if anxiety is distressing you and restricting your life, it really is worth making the effort to overcome it. The rewards will be substantial.

- Be prepared to invest time in doing the practical exercises – set aside 20 to 30 minutes each day if you can. You can maintain your achievements by practising your coping skills regularly and knowing how to learn from setbacks.

- Try to answer all the questions and do the exercises, even if you have to come back to some of them later. There may be times when you get stuck and can't think how to take things forward. If this happens, don't get angry with yourself or give up. Just put the book aside and come back to it later, when you are feeling more relaxed.

- You may find it helpful to work through the books with a friend. Two heads are often better than one. And you may be able to encourage each other to persist, even when one of you is finding it hard. Ask for the help of family and friends, particularly in the practical tasks.

- Re-read the workbook. You may get more out of it once you've had a chance to think about some of the ideas and put them into practice for a little while.

- Each workbook builds on what has already been covered. So what you learn when working with one will help you when you come to the next. It's quite possible simply to dip into different ones as you please, but you may get most out of the series if you follow them through systematically, step by step.

What if I don't feel better?

There is nothing to lose by working through this book; it will give you practical coping skills you can put into practice straight away. However, if you find that self-help alone is not meeting your needs (this is sometimes the case), see your family doctor, medical practitioner or specialist therapist, who can offer extra support. If you do need to seek more help this doesn't mean you have failed in any way; just that your difficulties are perhaps more complex.

A note of caution

These workbooks will not help everyone who has problem worries, fears and anxieties. If you find that focusing on anxiety is actually making you feel worse instead of better, you may be suffering from clinical depression. The recognized signs of clinical depression include:

- Constantly feeling sad, down, depressed or empty

- General lack of interest in what's going on around you

- A big increase or decrease in your appetite and weight

- A marked change in your sleep patterns

- Noticeable speeding up or slowing down in your movements and how you go about things

- Feeling of being tired and low in energy

- An intense sense of guilt or worthlessness

- Difficulty in concentrating and making decisions

- A desire to hurt yourself or a feeling that you might be better off dead

If you have had five or more of these symptoms (including low mood or loss of interest) for two weeks or more, you should seek professional help from a doctor, counsellor or psychotherapist. There is nothing shameful about seeking this sort of professional help – any more than there is anything shameful about taking your car to a garage if it is not working as it should, or going to see a lawyer if you have legal problems. It simply means taking your journey towards self-knowledge and self-acceptance with the help of a friendly guide, rather than striking out alone.

SECTION 1: What Is Anxiety?

Anxiety affects us all. It is not physically or mentally damaging. In most cases it is a normal response to a threatening situation; it can even be vital to survival. Anxiety is a normal reaction to stress or danger. It only becomes a problem when it is exaggerated or when you experience it in a situation that should not be threatening or alarming.

In the next two sections you will learn:

- The role of stress in anxiety

- Why it can be helpful to experience anxiety and what the effects of 'helpful' anxiety are

- What the effects of 'problem' anxiety are.

The stress response

Worry, fear and anxiety are crucial to our survival because they prepare us for coping with stress or danger. They trigger the release of a hormone (adrenaline) which in turn causes physical and mental changes. These prepare us for either taking on a challenge or escaping from a dangerous situation. Once the stress or danger has passed, these temporary changes gradually disappear.

Our ancestors were faced with very real threats to their safety, such as a wild animal or a hostile neighbour, so for them this immediate **fight or flight** response was very necessary. The stresses which we face today are less obvious: they can be delays, problems at home, deadlines or job loss. Even though these stresses are not a matter of life or death, we still experience the same reactions as did our ancestors.

Think about a recent experience you found stressful. Perhaps you had to give a presentation at work, or went to a party where you only knew one or two people. Write down the experience here:

_____

_____

_____

_____

Now read the list below and tick any of sensations or reactions you felt.

Physical changes

☐ Heart 'in throat'

☐ Heart racing

☐ Hair on back of neck standing on end

☐ Tense muscles

☐ Panting

☐ Sweating

☐ 'Butterflies' in the stomach

Changes in the way you thought or felt

☐ Extremely focused thinking

☐ Sudden or marked irritability

☐ Excitement

☐ Apparent slowing of time

☐ Anticipating a problem

Changes in the way you behaved

☐ Sudden burst of energy, speed or strength

☐ Being very still or 'frozen'

☐ Feeling shaky and exhausted after stress has passed

These symptoms are all signs of the stress response.

The physical changes

Release of adrenaline causes the following physical symptoms:

- increased muscular tension

- faster breathing

- higher blood pressure

- quicker heart beat

- more perspiration

- changes in the digestive system

- blood flowing to parts of the body which need extra energy.

All of these reactions increase our readiness for action and explain many of the physical sensations which we associate with anxiety, such as rapid breathing, heart racing and 'butterflies' in the stomach. This is the ideal state for someone who has to react with a burst of energy. If you were an athlete who was about to run an important race, for example, and you didn't experience these physical changes, you would be sluggish rather than ready for action.

Changes in the way you think or feel

When faced with danger or stress our thinking becomes more focused and there can be an improvement in concentration and problem-solving. This is an ideal state of mind for anyone facing a serious challenge. Imagine you were a surgeon carrying out an operation, a stockbroker needing to make a swift decision about an investment, or a parent restraining a child who is about to walk into the road. Without the stress response your reactions might be too careless.

We can also experience a range of emotional responses to stress, such as increased irritability or even a sense of well-being. This is why we sometimes become short-tempered in a stressful situation, feel exhilarated when a deadline is looming, or actually enjoy the anxiety caused by a horror film or rollercoaster ride.

Changes in the way you behave

The way we behave in reaction to stress or danger usually takes the form of either taking action to meet a challenge (fight) or escaping from the stressful situation (flight) and in some instances we 'freeze'. For example, if you see a tree branch falling towards you, you get a burst of energy and jump out of the way in order to escape. If you are driving and go into a skid, you become completely focused on correcting the skid and find the strength to hold on to the steering wheel. If you are suddenly shocked by something you might stand still: this can be a useful moment for reflection.

So the ways we respond to stress are normal, helpful and often vital. Up to a point, your performance levels actually increase as your stress levels get higher. This is shown in the diagram below. At the bottom-left of the line, you are relaxed but physically and mentally ill-equipped to deal with danger: you are not ready for action when you are in this state. As your stress levels rise, your body and mind become increasingly able to confront stress.

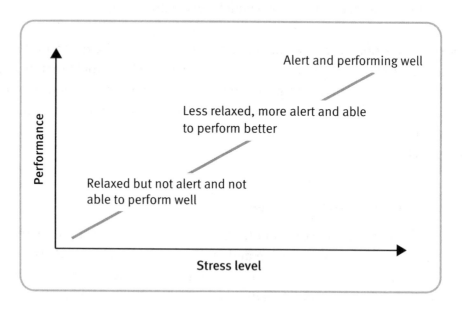

Stress and performance

Do you suffer from long-term stress?

Changes brought about by the stress response are helpful in the short term making us focused and ready for action. But problems can arise if the stress reaction is not switched off but continues: you can have too much of a good thing.

Work through this checklist of physical symptoms and check any that you experience regularly:

Physical changes

☐ Headaches

☐ Difficulty in swallowing

☐ Shoulder, neck and/or chest pain

☐ Stomach cramps

☐ Trembling/weak legs

☐ Heart pounding/palpitations

☐ Light-headedness

☐ Blurred vision

☐ Ringing in the ears

☐ Dizziness

☐ Nausea

☐ Shortness of breath

☐ Vomiting

☐ Diarrhoea

☐ Stomach pain

☐ Excessive/embarrassing sweating

☐ Fatigue

☐ Tingling in hands, feet or face

All of these symptoms are typical of someone experiencing long-term stress.

- The muscular tension so important for fight or flight can now develop into muscular discomfort throughout the body, including headaches, cramps, pain and tension.

- Raised blood pressure can cause a pounding heart, light-headedness, blurred vision and ringing in the ears.

- As breathing rate increases you might feel dizzy, nauseous and short of breath.

- If the digestive system is affected sickness, diarrhoea and stomach pain can result.

- Blood being redirected to the main muscles of the body can cause unpleasant skin sensations

Now look at the following list of changes in the way you think or feel and check any that apply to you.

Changes in the way you think or feel

☐ My thinking focuses only on worries or problems

☐ Problems seem impossible to solve

☐ My thoughts are always negative

☐ I'm always irritable

☐ I feel very fearful

☐ I've lost my self-confidence

☐ I feel hopeless

These symptoms are typical of someone suffering long-term stress. This way of thinking can become a vicious cycle when it's combined with the physical changes during stress. For example, if your heart races frequently this may lead to you think, 'I'm seriously ill – there's something wrong with my heart!' and become more anxious still.

Now think about the way you behave and tick any of the symptoms below that apply to you.

Changes in the way you behave

☐ I fidget all the time

☐ I stop eating properly

☐ I eat, smoke, drink or use drugs too much

☐ I avoid situations that might make me anxious

Constantly fidgeting can become exhausting, while eating too little or increased eating, smoking or drinking can take a toll on your health and well-being. Running away, or avoiding the situation or object which makes you anxious, is another common reaction to stress. But over time this may make you lose self-confidence so that the situation is even harder to face.

Long-term stress pushes you past peak performance, and instead performance begins to deteriorate. Michael's story below shows someone in the middle of this spiral. Underline anything in his story you relate to.

CASE STUDY: Michael

'I used to be positive about myself and had energy and ideas, but I've lost all that since we started to go through a crisis with the business. Now I really have to push myself to do routine things because I feel so tired and dull. Even when I get things done, I get no enjoyment from it and so everything feels like a chore. It doesn't end there because I go home worrying about the business and about my performance. I can't get these things out of my mind so I don't even try to be sociable any more. Sometimes I feel quite ill with it all and I haven't slept properly in months. I can't understand how I can push myself and not seem to get anywhere.'

The stress-distress cycle

As you can see the response to stress can itself become distressing. This might be because the physical changes are alarming. Or it might be because anxiety causes changes in the way we think or feel and affects our ability to cope. Perhaps a loss of self-confidence makes it difficult to face fears and overcome them. Whatever the reason, when the natural stress response causes more distress, a cycle has been created which is difficult to control (see the diagram below). This cycle, which maintains the stress response after it has been triggered, is the common factor in all forms of worry, fear and anxiety. We'll learn a lot more about the role of such cycles in anxiety in later sections.

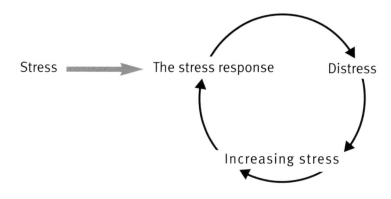

The stress-distress cycle

Summary

1 Anxiety is a normal, healthy response to stress in the short term.

2 Anxiety involves physical changes, changes to the way we think and feel and changes in the way we behave. These changes help to improve our performance in stressful situations.

3 Long-term or excessive stress causes long-term anxiety, which in turn causes unpleasant and unhelpful physical changes and changes in the way we think, feel and behave.

4 These changes can be stressful themselves, causing a vicious cycle of stress and distress.

What sta   times become a problem. The
stress re   n the stress and worsen the
anxiety.

- Physic   eart; these are caused by the
  physic

- Chang

- Ways i   or relieve anxiety

- Social   .... behaviour of other people

Often anxiety is maintained through a combination of these factors. The first step in breaking the cycles is to identify the ones that are at work in your particular case.

Physical symptoms that maintain a stress cycle

Physical responses to stress can begin a cycle of distress. Physical reactions such as a racing heart are a normal reaction to stress but some people misread their physical reaction and become more alarmed.

1 What physical reactions do you experience when you get stressed?

_____

_____

_____

2 How do these physical reactions make you feel? What emotions do you experience?

_____

_____

_____

_____

3 What thoughts or images run through your mind? What's the worst thing that could happen? Do you think that you might have a medical condition or be suffering some sort of attack, for example?

_____

_____

_____

_____

4 What happens when you have these thoughts? How do they make you feel? Do they change the physical symptoms you experience, making them worse or better?

_____

_____

_____

_____

The table below shows some typical physical reactions to stress, and the alarming thoughts they can trigger:

Physical reaction	Alarming thought
Muscular tension, especially around the chest	'This is a heart attack!'
Respiratory changes (panting)	'I can't breathe: I'll suffocate!'
Light-headedness	'I'm getting dizzy. I'll collapse. I'm having a stroke!'
Combination of symptoms	'I don't understand! I can't cope!'

The diagram below shows how this vicious cycle works:

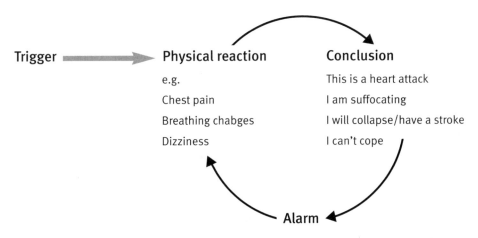

How physical reactions maintain stress

Fear of fear

If our physical reactions are extreme, anxiety can be very uncomfortable and frightening. Often this is enough to make a person fear anxiety: a fear of fear. When discomfort is expected or predicted – the fear of finding oneself in pain and struggling for breath, for example – the distress of the expectation can trigger an attack of anxiety or can drive a person to avoid situations where they predict being at risk.

CASE STUDY: Angie

Angie had been under a lot of stress: moving house, her youngest child was ill and then there was the pressure of work. Then, in a meeting she was put on the spot by her boss. She was quite thrown by the 'whoosh' of anxiety she experienced. She could not think straight and, physically, she felt almost in pain as her breathing became difficult. Quite quickly she realized that this was an anxiety attack, but it had been so disabling that she feared it happening again and she did everything she could to avoid it.

Self-fulfilling prophecies

Physical reactions to stress can maintain problems in other ways. The physical symptoms of shaking, sweating, nausea and faltering voice can affect a person's performance, particularly in public or social settings. Predicting that this will happen can undermine confidence, increase worries about performance and worsen the physical symptoms.

Read Stuart's story below and underline anything you relate to.

CASE STUDY: Stuart

Stuart, a college student, hates standing up in front of other people. Last term, as part of his course, he had to give a presentation to the rest of his group. Although he had pre-pared well and knew that the other students were friendly and supportive, he had been thinking ahead and was dreading the moment because he was so sure that it would go badly. When his turn came he could hardly stand up because his legs felt weak, and he was sweating. He was nervous and could only think how awful he was feeling. As he tried to read his paper, it was difficult to focus, so that he couldn't make out the words properly. Eventually the course leader asked him if he needed to sit down. Stuart was so embarrassed he couldn't even look at anyone else for the rest of the lesson. He has since vowed never to talk in public again.

If you have had an experience when physical sensations made things worse for you, describe it in the space below.

_____

_____

_____

_____

_____

_____

_____

_____

Ways of thinking that maintain a stress cycle

How we think can play a large role in maintaining our level of anxiety. We think not only in verbal terms (the thoughts that are like words running through our mind) but also visually. Sometimes our thinking reflects images that we see in our mind's eye, for example a fleeting picture of a road traffic accident or oneself suffering the humiliation of failure.

Many people who suffer from anxiety problems **overestimate** danger and **under-estimate** their ability to cope. For example, overestimating the dangers of driving and underestimating your driving skill could make you frightened to drive. Overestimating the difficulty of an examination and underestimating your ability to perform could make you anxious about sitting an exam.

Read the case study below and underline where Susan might be **overestimating** the difficulties she's facing. Use a wavy line to mark where she might **underestimate** her ability to cope.

CASE STUDY: Susan

Susan is running late for a very important meeting at work and can't find her car keys. She is getting increasingly stressed as time starts ticking by. These are the thoughts that run through her head: 'This is the one meeting all month that I can't afford to miss! What an idiot I am to mislay the keys. I'm always doing this kind of stupid thing. I'll never find them. If I miss this meeting everyone at work will think I'm hopeless, and I won't be able to give any convincing explanation for why I wasn't there. This could put my job at risk.' As Susan grows more worried she picks up bowls and cushions at random, unable to organize her search. Her tension levels rise further and all she can think about are the disastrous consequences of missing this now very important meeting. She is so focused on her growing fears that she misses the obvious – her partner, Bill, points out that the keys are in her pocket.

Are there situations where you overestimate problems, for example: 'This is the one meeting all month that I can't miss', or 'This could put my job at risk'? Are there situations where you underestimate your ability to cope, for example: 'What an idiot I am!', or 'I won't be able to give any convincing explanation…'? Make a note of them in the space below.

_____

_____

_____

_____

_____

_____

_____

_____

_____

_____

An anxious mind can be a distorting mind. When we're anxious we tend to focus on the negative, on the bad things that could happen. This is normal and is called *biased thinking*. As with all our anxious responses too much can be unhelpful: biased thinking can become unhelpfully distorted. The most common types of biased thinking are:

- Catastrophizing
- All-or-nothing thinking
- Exaggerating
- Ignoring the positive
- Scanning
- Worrying

As you read through the descriptions of each type of thinking below think if any apply to you.

Catastrophizing

This means predicting that the worst will happen. Examples of catastrophizing include receiving an official envelope and assuming that it contains a huge tax demand, or interpreting a scowl from a colleague as a sign that she hates you. Look at Susan's case study again and underline examples of catastrophizing.

Many people catastrophize about physical symptoms. For example, they see a headache as a sign of a stroke; chest pain means heart attack; skin tingling or numbness is interpreted as a sign of multiple sclerosis; a lump below the surface of the skin is believed to be cancer; a sore throat is believed to be the beginning of a bout of influenza ... which will stop you from completing the work you have lined up ... will mean that you never catch up with yourself ... and your reputation will be damaged for good!

In the space below write down some examples of when you predicted the worst only to find things didn't go as badly as you expected. Examples could be a job interview, an exam or a difficult meeting or phone call.

The event or situation	What I thought would happen	What actually did happen
Example: My boss asked me to see him first thing Monday morning	I was going to be laid-off	He offered me a promotion

All-or-nothing thinking

This is where you see everything in all-or-nothing terms rather than having a more balanced response: for example, 'I will always feel this badly,' rather than 'I feel bad at the moment but I could get better with help'; or 'everyone always picks on me,' rather than 'sometimes I am criticized and sometimes this is unjustified.' Look at Susan's story and highlight any examples of all-or-nothing thinking.

Another common form of all-or-nothing thinking is expecting perfection in yourself: 'If it isn't perfect, it isn't acceptable,' or 'this is not quite right: I have failed.' No one is perfect, certainly not all of the time. To expect this is to set yourself up for disappointment and further stress.

In the space below, write your attitude to different aspect of yourself. Is your outlook 'all or nothing' or more balanced?

Topic	All or nothing
Example: The way I look	I always look a mess
The way I look	
My job performance	
My relationships	
How I handle stress	

Exaggerating

This refers to exaggerating the negative or frightening aspects of your experiences: 'I really couldn't cope' (when in fact you have come through an incident); 'I almost threw up' (when stress had simply caused a feeling of nausea). This is closely linked to catastrophizing and all-or-nothing thinking. It is also linked to another thinking bias known as 'over-generalizing', where wide-reaching conclusions are drawn that aren't well supported by the evidence: for example, 'I'll never get a job', based on not being short listed for the first one you have applied for.

Look at the case study below and highlight the examples of exaggeration, all-or-nothing thinking, over-generalization and catastrophizing. Do not worry about distinguishing each type of bias as they do overlap; simply look for the unhelpful thinking styles.

CASE STUDY: Andrea

Andrea knows they are planning to lay off people at work, and she is having trouble sleeping because she is so anxious about her job. She is given a new project, and told she has been chosen as the right person to take responsibility for this important job. Her manager tells her she did excellent work on a similar project six months ago. This worries Andrea as she fears not being able to maintain her performance as she believes that her 'excellent work' was down to luck. The very first day she is to work on the project, she leaves one of the computer disks she needs at home. Immediately she panics, setting in motion a chain of thought: 'This is typical of me...I'm rubbish and every one will see it'... I can't be trusted with responsibility... my manager will brand me an incompetent... I'm bound to get the chop!"

Ignoring the positive

This means not paying attention to positive and reassuring facts and events, not taking on board compliments ('Oh this old thing'), not acknowledging achievements ('Oh anyone could have done that') and not recognizing personal strengths ('I didn't really do anything special; I'm not up to the job'). Ignoring the positive means picking out the negative and focusing on that. Read through Andrea's case study to find examples of this type of thinking.

Failure to recognize your good points and personal strengths undermines self-confidence, thus reducing a person's ability to cope with anxiety.

In the space below, try to recall some recent achievements or compliments you've received about your abilities. How easy is it to do this?

_____

_____

_____

_____

_____

_____

_____

_____

Scanning

This means searching for the thing that makes you anxious, for example looking for traffic if you are crossing the road; checking your body for aches and pains if you are worried about your health. Up to a point this can be helpful, but if exaggerated, it can actually inhibit you or increase the likelihood of scaring yourself. For example, scanning could prevent a person from crossing the road because they could not stop checking for traffic, or it could heighten a person's anxiety because we can all find aches and pains if we dwell on our bodies. Scanning can affect you in two ways: a) you are more likely to come across whatever it is that triggers your anxiety; b) you are likely to create false alarms for yourself.

A good example is a man with a spider phobia, compared to a woman without. The woman would probably walk into a room without noticing cobwebs, dusty corners or even any spiders, whereas the man with a spider phobia would immediately scan the room for all of these. When he noticed a strand of web, a shady corner or a crawling creature of some sort his fears would be confirmed. Ready to see the evidence he feared, he might also falsely interpret fluff on the carpet as a spider or a crack in the wall as a web.

In the space below write down some of the things that make you anxious. Then think of situations where you've practised scanning.

Anxiety trigger	Scanning behaviour
Example: I'm very anxious about ageing	*I not only study my face every day for any new line, I also find myself staring at the faces of friends and relatives, even actresses on television and at the cinema to compare myself*

Worrying

Worrying is a helpful response to anxiety – up to a point. It is the means by which we anticipate or review a problem and this often leads to a solution. For example, a person might worry that he will forget his computer disk – this prompts him to put it into his briefcase the night before his presentation, or a woman might dwell on a work problem and after a few minutes might see another perspective and come up with a solution. However, if worry does not lead to problem-solving, it tends to turn into cycles of unproductive and stressful thinking about a problem. Sometimes, unproductive worrying is maintained by beliefs about worrying: 'If I think about it, I will not be taken by surprise'; 'If I worry about it, it might not happen'; ' If I worry long enough, I'll find a solution.'

Consider Fran: before going on holiday she would anticipate and dwell on the things that could go wrong. She was far too anxious to be able to come up with solutions, but she felt that by worrying about the possible problems she was at least doing something constructive. But it was not constructive as she simply felt compelled to engage in a cycle of anxiety-provoking thinking which gave her no solution and a great deal of angst.

Mood changes

In addition to the thinking biases, negative mood changes caused by anxiety can further reduce our ability to deal with it. The experience of constant anxiety can create a sense of hopelessness and misery. These then undermine our coping abilities. This is one reason why it is so important to learn how to catch problem anxiety as early as possible.

Irritability, which is often linked to stress, can also fuel anxiety. This mood can easily have a negative effect on work performance or social behaviour, thus creating even more worries.

The case study below shows the effect of negative mood. Look also for examples of scanning.

CASE STUDY: Nick

Nick hasn't had a serious girlfriend for three years, and, although he very much wants to meet someone, he has become more and more anxious that there's something about him that puts off women. He now feels hopeless as well as scared. His friends take him to lots of parties, but he is pessimistic, self-conscious and awkward, and he always falls into the same pattern of behaviour. Although he makes an initial effort, he soon gives up, takes a back seat, and drinks alone. As he looks around the room he sees other men chatting easily to women and concludes that the problem is all to do with him. If a woman does strike up a conversation with him his first thought is that it will not last and that she will find him boring. He constantly looks for signs that she is bored, and this makes it almost impossible for him to overcome his anxiety.

Think about a situation where your mood affected your ability to manage your anxieties. Describe it in the space below.

_____

_____

_____

_____

_____

_____

_____

_____

_____

_____

Ways of behaving that maintain a stress cycle

The natural response to anxiety is to take action to reduce it – in other words, to do something to gain comfort or calm. Unfortunately some of these responses do not help to overcome anxiety in the long run, and could even make it worse.

Go through the following checklist and tick anything that applies to you.

☐ **1** I stay in often; apart from when I absolutely have to, I hardly leave the house now at all

☐ **2** I avoid public places; I find I feel quite unnerved and edgy in crowded or busy places

☐ **3** I avoid cramped, confined or crowded places

☐ **4** I seem to be avoiding social situations more often

☐ **5** I've been avoiding new places, people or experiences

☐ **6** I make sure I stay out of any arguments or conflicts at work or at home

☐ **7** I find I'm relying on close friends for advice and support more than I ever used to

☐ **8** I've actually run away from a situation, place, or event that made me uncomfortable

☐ **9** I've been restricting myself to places, people or experiences I am used to; anything out of the norm makes me anxious

☐ **10** I've been drinking too much alcohol lately

☐ **11** I've been drinking tea/coffee too much lately

☐ **12** I've been needing a cigarette more frequently

☐ **13** I've been comfort eating

☐ **14** I've become dependent on drugs to get me through

Points 1 to 9 are clear examples of avoidance or escape, probably the two most natural behavioural responses to anxiety – avoiding whatever causes you anxiety or attempting to get yourself out of the situation.

Avoidance and escape

Sometimes the way we avoid or escape from something is obvious. For example, if you never go into a shopping mall because you feel overwhelmed by crowds, or you walk in only to race out again, you are avoiding or escaping from your problem.

Sometimes the way we behave is less obvious. For example, you might be prepared to enter the shopping mall, but only when accompanied by a friend or after taking tranquillizers. Or you might go into the mall but quickly find help from someone in the centre or call a friend to ask for support. In this way, you never learn that it is possible to face your fear without help, and so the original fear remains intact.

Think about ways in which you might be avoiding your fear. Write them in the space below.

_____

_____

_____

_____

_____

_____

_____

_____

_____

_____

If you ticked points 10 to 14 in the questionnaire you may be using food, drink or drugs to control your anxiety. This also means you are avoiding the problem and this can be even more unhelpful in the long run. Cigarettes, coffee or tea, and chocolate are all **stimulants**. They cause chemical changes in your body encouraging the release of adrenaline, the stress hormone, together with all its effects of tremors, palpitations and others (see page 2 for more information). Many people find they have tremors or palpitations after drinking too much coffee, for example; this will further increase discomfort, which could trigger worrying thoughts and perhaps impair performance.

Turning to alcohol is also unhelpful. Although it can be relaxing in the short term, it becomes a **stimulant** when it is broken down in your body. You might have already experienced this double effect of alcohol on those evenings when you have unwound with a drink or two only to find that you woke in the night, restless and unable to get back to sleep.

If you use food, drugs or alcohol as a long-term coping strategy, you may find the physical changes which result, such as gaining weight, fatigue and ill health, will worsen your stress levels and increase your anxiety. If you are using these substances to avoid anxiety, they will prevent you from facing fear and learning how to meet the challenge of difficult situations.

Seeking reassurance

It is very common to seek out advice and help from friends, family or professionals when we are worried or afraid. 'Do you think that he dislikes me?'; 'Do you think that I have remembered everything?'; 'What do you think this lump is?' This is helpful if used it to develop better ways to deal with concerns – for example, using it to look at the cause of your anxieties and get a different view on them.

The key to using reassurance is to use the new knowledge to change your perspective so that you feel more confident and can *assure yourself* from now on. However, if you are not able to do this, you will only gain temporary relief from taking the advice of others and you will find yourself having to seek reassurance again.

It is possible to become increasingly dependent on seeking more reassurance and less able to face and tackle the real issues. To make matters worse, friends, family and professionals can grow tired of being asked for reassurance, and this can strain relationships and give rise to more anxiety.

Do you find that you repeatedly seek reassurance? If so, use the space below to write down from whom you seek reassurance and why.

_____

_____

_____

_____

_____

_____

Social situations that maintain stressful cycles

Stressful life events can increase the risk of developing an anxiety problem. And stressful situations that seem to be outside our control, such as looking after young children, poor health, difficult work environments, ongoing problems at home, long-term unemployment and financial pressures, can play a role in maintaining anxiety. It is important to recognize to what extent external factors might be contributing to your difficulties. It is not always possible to change or avoid difficult circumstances; therefore, it is important to develop a range of stress management skills so you can handle pressure whenever and wherever it occurs.

Think about what is happening in your life at the moment. Write down any events that you are finding particularly stressful. Are there stresses which you can eliminate or reduce?

_____

_____

_____

_____

_____

_____

_____

Other people

The actions of other people can also play an important role in maintaining your anxiety, in both obvious and subtle ways.

● People can criticize you, bully, put pressure on you, be insulting and undermining. This is an obvious stress.

● However, people can also maintain your anxiety in less obvious ways, even when the person is well-meaning. Look at the two case studies below and think about how the anxiety sufferer's partner or friend may be maintaining their anxiety. Write your answer in the space below.

_____

_____

_____

_____

_____

_____

_____

CASE STUDY: Doreen

For many years Doreen has been anxious about leaving her home, and especially fright-ened of crowded places such as supermarkets. She finds going shopping very difficult. She used to struggle out to the local shop once a week, but last year her sister moved to a house just around the corner. Now she visits every day to check on Doreen, and brings her shopping whenever she needs it. Doreen never has to leave the house at all, and says she is much calmer as a result.

Is Doreen's sister helpful or unhelpful?

CASE STUDY: Simon

Simon is very anxious about developing cancer. His mother and brother both developed cancer at his age and he is constantly asking his doctor for x-rays and blood tests to check his health status. His doctor has carried out all the necessary checks and has assured Simon that he is in good health. However, Simon is not convinced. His wife, Sally, has bought him several books on cancer prevention and has changed their diet along the lines these books suggest. In an effort to calm him down she checks him reg-ularly for any unusual growths or tumours and sympathizes with him when he com-plains that his doctor isn't taking him seriously. Simon says he'd be lost without her support.

Is Sally helpful or unhelpful?

Summary

1 There are several types of 'anxious thinking' to look out for.

2 One types involves overestimating danger and underestimating your ability to cope.

3 Once the anxiety response has been triggered it can be maintained and even worsened by 'maintaining cycles'.

4 Maintaining cycles can be fuelled by physical factors, the way we think or feel, the way we behave and social situations.

5 Several different maintaining cycles may be operating at the same time.

6 When you can recognize the cycles that maintain your worries, fears and phobias, you can start to think about breaking them. Parts Two and Three cover practical ways of doing this.

SECTION 3: Why Do People Have Problems with Anxiety?

Worries, fears and anxieties affect everyone differently. Anyone who experiences problems with fears, phobias and anxieties will ask 'Why me?' It is important to answer this question if you want to take control of your problems in the long term.

There are several different reasons why someone might be more at risk of developing anxiety problems. They are:

- Personality type
- Family history
- Life stresses
- Coping skills and style
- Social support

Work through the following section to see which of the risk factors may apply to you. In many cases of anxiety problems, there is more than one risk factor at work.

Personality type

There are many dimensions of personality, including introvert/extrovert; optimist/pessimist; easygoing/'driven'. We each exhibit differing degrees of characteristics but there are indications that being at an extreme position on such dimensions could render a person vulnerable. For example, the more driven and competitive characters might be more prone to stress symptoms because they push themselves hard, while the 'worriers' amongst us might be prone to anxiety.

However, personality traits are only one factor that might contribute to anxiety or stress and there is evidence that even the vulnerable can learn to change their behaviour and outlook so as to minimize the likelihood of developing problems.

Family history

We are all born with certain fears, for example of strangers, heights, snake-like objects, 'creepy-crawlies' and being left alone. From a survival point of view an infant who cries when held by a stranger, or who screams as a spider crawls towards him, is more likely to survive than a baby who doesn't react. In time the child learns not to over-react to these triggers, although some individuals do carry the fears into adulthood. This suggests that fears can be encoded in our genes, and there is the possibility that anxiety can be passed on in families.

Does anxiety run in families?

Studies have shown that anxiety disorders can run in families, although it is difficult to know whether this is because of an inherited a 'gene for anxiety' or because of the way a person was brought up. For instance, an overprotective father's constant warnings that dogs bite could make his son more likely to develop a fear of dogs.

Does anyone in your family suffer from anxiety-related problems?

_____

_____

_____

It is important to remember that, even though there might be strong trends in families, it is possible to overcome fears or tendencies to worry.

Life stresses

Life events can often bring about emotional problems. Both depression and anxiety are related to 'stressful' events. We all understand that 'loss' events such as divorce or a death in the family can result in depression, while anxiety is linked to 'threat' events: unknown exam results; an undiagnosed medical problem; the risk of redundancy, for example.

An event does not have to be unpleasant to be experienced as 'stressful'. Anything that forces you to make changes or adjust to a new situation can cause stress and therefore contribute to anxiety.

Go through the list on the next page and check any of the life events that have happened to you in the last few years. In the space at the bottom, write down any events that you think might be important, but which aren't on the list as the list is not comprehensive.

☐ Serious accident or injury

☐ Alcoholism or other substance dependency in the family

☐ Sudden financial demand (e.g. tax demand)

☐ Ongoing money problems

☐ Sudden severe illness

☐ Chronic illness of any severity

☐ Sexual problem

☐ Job worries (e.g. redundancy or fear of redundancy)

☐ Starting a new job (including promotion)

☐ Marital or relationship problems

☐ Family unhappiness or arguments

☐ Marriage

☐ Having children

☐ Moving house

☐ Exams/tests

☐ Children leaving home

☐ Being the victim of crime

☐ Moving to a new town or country

☐ Retirement

☐ Trouble with the law

Others

_____

_____

_____

_____

How big an effect did the event have?

To appreciate how great an effect life events might have had on you, go through the list again and look at those that you have ticked or added. Consider each event: did one event result in even more changes? For example:

- changes to your financial situation, your habits and hobbies, your location

- changes to your way of thinking (for example how you think about yourself, your relationships and your outlook on the future)

- physical changes (for example limits on your mobility, changes to the way you look).

Remember that major life events often cluster, for example, a marriage is likely to be linked with a house move, or redundancy to a financial crisis, which can lead to greater feelings of stress.

Childhood events

If an experience in your life in recent years matches a distressing experience from your childhood you may react with high anxiety. Your childhood reaction can make you overestimate the danger of the current event and underestimate your ability to cope. Look at June's case study for clues about how life history can increase the impact of a stressful event.

CASE STUDY: June

When June's husband Alfie was diagnosed with angina he wasn't too worried and simply decided to take better care of himself. June, however, was very anxious. She worried about him all day, and couldn't help bursting into tears whenever she discussed his condition. At night she had trouble sleeping because fears and worries would go round and round in her head. Alfie tried to talk to her about it calmly, but soon her anxiety began to test his patience. Finally he managed to get June to sit down and talk through the issue and it turned out that she was thinking about her own parents, both of whom had died of heart problems within a few months of each other when she was a teenager. Now that they both understood why she was so worried, June and Alfie were able to talk about his angina sensibly and sensitively. He assured her that he took her anxieties seriously, and she was reassured that Alfie was looking after his health and was in no immediate danger.

Think back to your childhood. Do you have powerful memories of being extremely frightened or believing that you were in grave danger? Write them down here.

_____

_____

_____

_____

_____

_____

_____

_____

_____

_____

_____

_____

Look at what you have written about your childhood fears and see if any events in your current life seem to match.

Your way of thinking and feeling

Earlier, we saw how ways of thinking such as catastrophizing can trigger anxiety and keep it going. Anyone with a tendency towards this type of thinking is going to be more at risk of developing problems than the person whose outlook is more balanced.

The way we see ourselves and the world is also influenced by our mood. So for example, a businessman might well see himself as masterful in a world of welcome challenges when his life is going well and he is feeling positive. If he becomes unhappy and pessimistic, he might begin to anticipate failure and he might become fearful of the very same work tasks which he previously welcomed. Anxious and depressed people are more likely to think in distorted ways. When this happens, as we have seen, anxiety can start perpetuating itself.

Coping skills and style

People react to stress and anxiety in their own individual way, through the use of *coping skills*. Some coping skills are effective – for instance, facing up to problems and working out how to solve them. Others are less helpful – for instance, constantly avoiding anxiety-provoking situations, or comfort eating. Read through the scenarios below and select the coping skill that you usually use.

1 Troubling thoughts and nagging anxiety mean that you can't sleep. What do you do?

☐ **a** Lie in bed looking at the clock and worrying that you'll be tired tomorrow.

☐ **b** Get up and have an alcoholic night cap.

☐ **c** Get up and engage in something distracting but calming – for example do some knitting or write out a shopping list for tomorrow.

2 Your anxieties have got the better of you and you decide you can't face going to the party you were supposed to be attending. What do you do instead?

☐ **a** Sit at home but imagine what everyone at the party is saying about you.

☐ **b** Raid the fridge.

☐ **c** Lose yourself in a good book: you have sent your apologies so there is no use in dwelling on it.

3 You've got to make a difficult phone call but you've been putting it off all week. How do you tackle it?

☐ **a** Decide that just thinking about it is making you feel ill, so it's better if you put it off until next week.

☐ **b** Take a tranquillizer before picking up the phone.

☐ **c** Draw up a list of the points you want to make, and rehearse the possible objections that might be raised and how you will respond to them.

How did you answer?

If you chose **a** or **b** in any of the cases you may have adopted an unhelpful coping strategy, namely excessive worrying or avoidance. These ways of coping with anxiety can actually reinforce fears. Excessive worrying keeps anxiety alive without providing a solution and avoidance stops us from mastering our fears (See earlier parts on avoidance and worrying.)

There are many reasons why people develop unhelpful coping styles. Perhaps the strategies are simply easier to fall back on (comfort eating or avoidance, for example) or perhaps more helpful techniques were never learnt.

Parts Two and Three will help you to develop new coping strategies. You will be less likely to rely on techniques which are not going to help you in the long term and which could even make your difficulties worse.

Social support

The less social support we have the more at risk we are of developing emotional problems, including anxiety. The greater the social support the more protected we are against trauma and ongoing stresses. You may have one or more particularly close and confiding friendships or a wide network of supportive contacts. This will be protective and is particularly important at times of major life events and life crises.

It is important to try to ensure you maintain your existing friendships, however anxious you may feel, or however little you may feel like socializing. Friends and relationships can definitely help you manage your anxiety better.

Look at the box over the page. You can understand how your anxiety problem arose in the first place by thinking about your personal risk factors and risks because of your social situation. Think about the ways in which your anxiety is maintained because of your coping style and ongoing stressful events in your life.

Why me? What makes me vulnerable?

For example, personality traits

_____

_____

_____

Why now? What triggered my anxiety?

For example, a particular event or series of stresses

_____

_____

_____

Why isn't it going away? What circumstances, thinking styles and coping styles maintain my problem?

For example, ongoing stresses, exaggerated thinking, coping by avoiding.

_____

_____

_____

Summary

1 Risk factors for anxiety include personality type, personal history, life stresses, coping skills and style and social support.

2 Risk factors often act in combination to make you more, or less, vulnerable to anxiety-related problems.

3 Distressing events in your childhood may match events in your present life and trigger anxiety.

SECTION 4: What Kinds of Anxiety Disorders Are There?

Everyone experiences worry, fear and anxiety differently. It is very important that you reflect on and understand what they mean to you personally. Although the experience of anxiety is a very personal one, professionals have recognized that some fears and anxieties have shared features. Here are the most common types of anxiety problems:

- Phobia – a fear of a particular thing which is so intense that a person avoids it, for example a fear of dogs or a fear of flying

- Panic attack – intense feelings of fear or a sense of a looming disaster combined with powerful physical reactions such as breathlessness or chest pains

- Generalized anxiety disorder – a persistent feeling of anxiety making you feel like you are suffering constant physical and mental discomfort

- Obsessive-compulsive disorder – a compulsion to carry out particular activities or to dwell on certain images or thoughts in order to feel at ease; for example some people need to wash their hands repeatedly for fear of catching a germ or being infected

- Health anxiety – extreme anxiety about real or imagined health problems

- Post-traumatic stress disorder – a prolonged stress reaction following an unusually traumatic event such as a serious road accident.

Phobias

Specific fears are common, but they become a problem – a phobia – when they become so intense that they lead to avoidance of a particular thing or situation and affect quality of life.

Some intense fears are very healthy – it is natural to be frightened of a dog growling and frothing at the mouth. And some intense fears do not affect our day-to-day life. A phobia about climbing a ladder might not be a problem if you are never likely to have to do this – however, it is a very real problem for a house painter.

How phobias are maintained

Problem phobias are maintained because of overestimation of risk and avoidance. This stops a person from testing out the reality of the fear and also prevents the development of coping skills that would improve confidence in facing the phobia.

Phobias can be sorted into general categories. The main ones are simple phobia, social phobia and agoraphobia.

Types of simple phobia

Simple phobias involve fear of a specific object or situation, such as fear of wasps or fear of heights. It is important to realize that almost anything can become an object of intense fear for a person. Someone with a simple phobia may feel extreme anxiety about the idea or image of the object – a picture of a dog might be enough to cause extreme anxiety; the dog doesn't have to be physically near. Here are some examples of phobias that many people experience. Their medical names are based on the feared object or situation and are from ancient Greek.

- **Claustrophobia – fear or being closed in or trapped**. People who are claustrophobic often find it difficult or impossible to ride in lifts or travel on underground trains.

- **Acrophobia – fear of heights**. Someone with a fear of heights might find it hard to climb an open staircase or stand at the edge of a lookout.

- **Aerophobia – fear of flying**. Many people don't like flying but if you have a phobia you might experience such intense feelings of anxiety about flying that it will be almost impossible for you to get on to a plane.

- **Arachnophobia – fear of spiders**. Again, this is a common fear but someone with arachnophobia might be so distressed by spiders that even a picture or thought of a spider could make them feel extremely anxious.

- **Ophidophobia – fear of snakes**. Another common fear with similar consequences to arachnophobia.

- **Haematophobia – fear of blood**. Most fears trigger a rise in blood pressure, but blood phobia is associated with a drop in blood pressure so that a person might literally pass out on seeing blood.

- **Hydrophobia – fear of water**. Someone suffering from a fear of water might find it impossible to ever learn how to swim.

Read the case study below. If you suffer from a phobia you may understand a lot of the feelings Geoff describes. Underline any points in his story that you relate to.

CASE STUDY: Geoff

'It might seem silly, and my family certainly thinks it is, but I go to pieces when I see a cat – even if it's only a picture of one. It sets my stomach churning and my heart racing and I think, "I have just got to get away, I can't handle this!" and then I run.

'I have been like this since I was three or four years old and I saw two cats fighting. They were all bloody and then one turned and looked at me. I was terrified. I am very careful not to go into areas where I might see a cat. I don't visit anyone without first checking whether they or their neighbours own a cat. I don't browse in card shops – do you realize how many greeting cards have cats on them? I'm glad that I'm a man and I get sent ships and trains at birthdays! Although I'm joking a bit now, it's no joke if I see a cat, or if I think I've seen a cat. It really affects my day-to-day life and I am restricted in what I can do and where I can go. It's getting worse, rather than better as time goes on.'

If you have a phobia, use the space below, describe your fear, how you think it began and the affect it has on your life now.

_____

_____

_____

_____

_____

_____

_____

_____

_____

_____

If you suffer from a phobia you will learn ways to overcome your fear in Parts Two and Three.

Social phobias

Social phobias are different from simple phobias. People with social phobia fear not just one specific thing but a range of situations where they might be exposed to being judged by others. Having to give a presentation at work is an example of this, or having to give a speech at a wedding. However, it doesn't have to be a formal performance: some people become very anxious just attending a party or social gathering where they think others will be looking at them.

How social phobias are maintained

People who suffer social phobia tend to predict and fear that others will judge them and think bad thoughts about them. They also tend to be very self-focused, which limits their ability to get a wider perspective of the situation. This fear can then undermine performance, and even promote avoidance, which then feeds into a cycle of worry.

Read Stella and Brian's case studies and underline anything that you relate to.

CASE STUDY: Stella

'I was once quite outgoing and thought that I was confident. That all changed with my first pregnancy. I put on a lot of weight – much more than I should have, but I didn't mind because I was pleased about the baby and I thought that the weight would disappear after the birth. Partly because I was so huge, we did not socialize much in the late stages of the pregnancy – I just didn't have the energy or the inclination to go out. We did go to a family wedding and I remember finding it quite hard work to mix and chat – but I decided that this was because I was tired.

'After my daughter was born, I was overweight, a bit depressed and very tired. I no longer felt confident in myself and I had the most unpleasant time at the baby's baptism. I couldn't find it in me to be cheerful and then I overheard someone say: "What has happened to Stella, she used to be so lively and attractive?" That just crushed any confidence that I had left and I wouldn't go out for weeks. I was so miserable that I couldn't get rid of the weight and that made me feel worse about meeting others. Now my little girl is five, I am still overweight and I still can't face going to social events unless I have some false courage in the form of a drink. It is painful not being able to think of anything other than how pitiful I am and how others are judging me. I do make myself attend my daughter's school events but I dread them and I keep myself to myself once I'm there. When I can, I persuade my husband to go instead of me.'

CASE STUDY: Brian

'The larger the gathering, the worse it is. Ever since I forgot my lines in a school play and everyone laughed, I have been terrified of public speaking. I know it seems ridiculous – I was an eight-year-old schoolboy then and I am a manager now – but I still feel just as frightened as I did at school. I get clammy hands and I feel my throat tighten and my mind often goes blank or is beset by worries. I feel so self-conscious and worry that I am making a fool of myself or that the audience will think that I'm stupid. I cope by doing my best to delegate public speaking to other people and swallowing the odd tranquillizer. Sadly, it is just impossible for me to chair meetings and give presentations and my career is suffering, which makes me very nervous.'

In the space below describe your own experience of social phobia if you suffer from it and how you think is affecting your life.

_____

_____

_____

_____

_____

_____

_____

_____

_____

_____

_____

_____

_____

Parts Two and Three will give you strategies to help you overcome social phobia.

Agoraphobia

Agoraphobia is a common problem. It is not simply a fear of open spaces; it is the fear of leaving a place of safety and being exposed to perceived threats or dangers. A person may feel safe at home, in their car or at the doctor's surgery, but fear that something terrible will happen if they venture outside these 'secure' areas.

How agoraphobia is maintained

Agoraphobia is maintained by avoidance. This can be very obvious avoidance such as not leaving a safe base or a subtle avoidance such as relying on alcohol or another person to help. It is often associated with panic attacks (see below), triggered by powerful fear. The panic then becomes associated with leaving a safe base and it becomes even more difficult to venture out.

Read Linda's story below and underline anything you relate to.

CASE STUDY: Linda

'I have not been out of the house for six months. I did go to see my doctor at Christmas, but I got into such a state that I nearly collapsed and now I get him to see me here. I feel safe here and I don't get the awful feelings, but I'm not even relaxed at home if I know a stranger is visiting. I often have a drink to calm me if the paperboy is coming to collect the paper money or the gas man is coming to read the meter. Sometimes, though, I just refuse to answer the door.

'I was always a bit nervous about going out and about and gradually, I went to fewer and fewer places on my own and I began to rely more and more on a glass or two of sherry to give me Dutch courage. A year ago I was able to use the corner shop and to get round the block to see my sister but I can't do that now – even with the sherry. Just talking about it make me feel wobbly and breathless. I try not to think about the awful feelings I get – thinking about them makes me feel almost as bad as going out does. Sometimes I wonder if I'm going mad. My sister is very helpful, though – she does my shopping and visits me nearly every day.'

If you suffer from agoraphobia, use the space below to describe your own feelings and how it affects your life.

_____

_____

_____

_____

_____

_____

_____

_____

_____

_____

_____

_____

_____

Parts Two and Three will give you strategies to help you overcome agoraphobia.

Panic attacks

The term 'panic attack' describes intense feelings of fear or looming disaster. This is combined with a very powerful physical reaction. A sufferer may find herself fighting for breath, experiencing chest pains, unable to see clearly and feeling very frightened. An attack can come on very rapidly.

Overbreathing, that is rapid, shallow breathing or _hyperventilation_, is a common reaction during panic and it produces even more distressing physical symptoms, such as dizziness, tingling beneath the skin, muscle pain and ringing in the ears.

There can be a wide range of triggers for a panic attack, for example being faced with a fear and not feeling able to cope; a chest pain incorrectly believed to be a heart attack; or dizziness wrongly perceived as a stroke.

How panic is maintained

Panic frequently occurs in combination with other anxiety disorders. It is often maintained by a tendency to jump to frightening conclusions, by misinterpretations, and by overestimating danger. Such frightening thoughts increase anxiety levels which then worsen the symptoms of anxiety (including hyperventilation) and this can further increase anxiety until it develops into a panic attack. Coping by avoiding the triggers for a panic attack only makes things worse because this undermines self-confidence which then fuels fear.

Read Mark's story below and underline anything you relate to.

CASE STUDY: Mark

'I will never forget the first time I had a panic attack – I thought I was dying! I was working on a stressful project and had got really hyped up on black coffee and very little else that day. By the evening, I was running late and knew that I'd have to rush to get to Renee's on time. Of course, the traffic was bad and in the back of the taxi I found myself getting more stressed and then I became hot and dizzy and I could hardly breathe. Somehow I paid the driver, but in the apartment I seemed to lose all control. I was sweating, gasping for breath, I had pains in my chest and my vision was getting dim. I couldn't hear what Renee was saying because of a ringing in my ears, but she had called a doctor because we both thought that I was having a heart attack. The doctor said that I had had a panic attack and that it was probably caused by the day's stress. This should have reassured me – and it did for a day or two – but then I had another and, again, I couldn't get in control of the situation. Although I tell myself that these are not heart attacks and that they cannot harm me, I am now so frightened of the experience that I'm always worried by the slightest unpleasant physical sensation and I avoid places where I've had them.'

If you have experienced panic attacks, use the space below to describe them and how they affect your life.

_____

_____

_____

_____

_____

_____

_____

Parts Two and Three will give you strategies to help you overcome panic attacks.

Generalized anxiety disorder (GAD)

People with generalized anxiety disorder have persistent, sometimes overwhelming feelings of anxiety. These cause what seems like constant physical and mental discomfort. Many people with GAD say things like: 'I never seem to be free of worry,' or 'I can never relax, something is always troubling me. I am constantly on edge.'

In addition, sufferers might experience periods of intense anxiety, which often seem to come 'out of the blue'. The chronic worry associated with GAD is both physically and emotionally draining.

How GAD is maintained

GAD seems to develop because a person experiences an enormous number of worries or they perceive a wide range of situations as threatening. A hallmark of the condition is worrying, which we have seen can be an unproductive and unfruitful activity. Worrying tends to raise anxiety levels, which can then render a person more prone to worrying and therefore more likely to continue to suffer from GAD.

It can be helpful to tease out the collection of fears associated with GAD in order to tackle them individually.

Read Claire's story below and underline anything you relate to.

CASE STUDY: Claire

'I always worry and I never relax nowadays. There is never a moment when I am free of aches and tension and my mind is almost always focused on worries, although sometimes I can't even put my finger on just what worries me. I simply have a 'sense' of things going badly. It makes me so tired and irritable and I have not been able to sleep or work properly and have not felt well in months.

'It seems to have crept up on me over the last year or two. Others have always said that I was highly strung but this was never a problem – I just seemed to have more "nervous energy" than most and I used this to my advantage. If anything, I should be more relaxed now that the children have gone to university, the recession seems to be coming to an end and my husband and I have more time to spend together. Instead, I'm even more edgy than usual – I worry about the children coping independently, about the next recession and then I get no pleasure from the time I spend with my husband. Perhaps I haven't got enough to occupy my mind, I don't know.

'I saw my doctor who said that I should join a yoga class and learn to unwind – I tried but I found it impossible to concentrate and I ended up getting more and more irritable! Now I try to cope by keeping busy in the shop, but this isn't easy because I am so tired that I can't seem to concentrate so I make silly mistakes and that stresses me and winds me up even more. I feel so hopeless that I just can't imagine when this is going to end.'

If you suffer from GAD, use the space below to describe your feelings and how they affect your life.

_____

_____

_____

_____

_____

_____

_____

_____

_____

_____

_____

_____

Parts Two and Three will give you strategies to help you overcome generalized anxiety disorder.

Obsessive-compulsive disorder (OCD)

People who have obsessive-compulsive disorder feel compelled to carry out particular acts or to dwell on certain images or thoughts in order to feel at ease. Often their compulsions are driven by anxieties about their own health or their family's, about safety and security or about hygiene. For example, a person might feel compelled to hand wash repeatedly in order to avoid catching a germ or might check over and over again that doors and windows are locked to make sure the house is safe. Or a sufferer might feel compelled to dwell on a mental image of the family being safe and well or compelled to repeat specific and reassuring phrases in order to reassure themselves.

There is a chain of reactions in OCD:

1 perceiving a threat

2 this triggers a worrying thought or image

3 this drives the compulsion to perform a comforting or reassuring activity

4 in the short term this is soothing or comforting: in the long term the fears remain unchallenged.

Some sufferers describe OCD as the most embarrassing of the anxiety disorders and many individuals who are troubled by it will never disclose their problem. Yet responding to a worrying thought or image is a useful response if it is not exaggerated. Imagine that you are leaving your house and you think:

'Did I switch off the gas fire? It would be dangerous to leave it on all day.'

This might then concern you enough to go back and check.

Or think of the father who, when driving home, sees a cyclist without lights being knocked off her bicycle: this triggers an unpleasant image of his own children being injured and prompts him to check that they have working lights when they go out at night.

These reactions are useful but they would be a problem if you felt compelled to return several times to check your house, or were constantly plagued by frightening images of your children and became overprotective to reassure yourself.

How OCD is maintained

People usually cope with OCD by avoiding anything that might trigger their anxieties, or by engaging in response which gives them swift reassurance. Unfortunately this then keeps the problem going because the person with OCD fails to learn that things will be okay. For example, someone might return to the house twenty times to avoid the discomfort of worrying about a possible fire; or someone might restrict the behaviour of children to avoid worrying about their welfare. The person never learns that fears are unfounded or bearable and so the fears remain unchallenged and intact.

Read Malcolm's story below and underline anything you relate to.

CASE STUDY: Malcolm

'I never worried much until I was in the army. We saw so many awful things and witnessed so many personal disasters that I think that we all became a bit superstitious about things. I can remember that I would double and triple check my equipment so that I took no extra risks. Once I left the army, I gradually gave up a lot of my obsessive checking and I've never had a problem with it. That is until six months ago.

'It was around that time that I set a retirement date. Knowing that I only had another year with the firm, my boss suddenly promoted me to an executive position with a lot more responsibility – particularly financial. He said that he wanted to send me off with a good bonus and a recognition of my abilities. That was a nice gesture but it increased my stress levels. I found myself worrying more and more about the safety of the office. I would travel home wondering if I had locked my office, locked the safe, set the burglar alarm, and so on. Very soon I could picture the safe being broken into because I hadn't checked everything and then I saw myself shamed in front of the man who had trusted me with this extra responsibility. By now I was so worried that I would return to the office time after time to check the safe, to check my office and to check the alarm. I could do this as many as twenty times and I began getting home later and later and more and more upset. My wife says that she can't stand much more of this.'

If you suffer from OCD, use the space below to describe your experience and how it affects your life.

Parts Two and Three will give you strategies to help you overcome obsessive-compulsive disorder.

Physical problems

We've already looked at some of the physical symptoms caused by stress and anxiety. Sometimes such symptoms are the first sign that you are overstressed. Typical physical symptoms include:

- difficulty in sleeping

- stomach and digestive problems

- headaches

- raised blood pressure

- worsened asthma

- difficulty in swallowing

- nausea and diarrhoea.

How physical problems are maintained

Stress can both cause and maintain these conditions. For example a child might have nausea and diarrhoea because pressures at school cause her stress, and this physical response could then cause her additional worry which would maintain the stress and sickness. Or a man might discover that he has developed high blood pressure and be so concerned by this that his anxiety levels increase and further raises his blood pressure.

Read Amanda's story below and underline anything you relate to.

CASE STUDY: Amanda

'It's all very well for my doctor to say "Just relax and then you'll find that you sleep better," but she's not the one who is tossing and turning for hours, worrying that another night of poor sleep is going to make the next day hell. I'm a teacher and I find it impossible to control a classroom full of children if I am feeling exhausted, and that's how I feel every day. I do avoid coffee now but it doesn't help much because I have reached the point where I am on edge all of the time. I dread going to bed because I know I won't sleep properly and then I can predict that I won't be able to cope well the next day at school. Knowing this winds me up so much that the last thing I'm able to do is relax!'

If you experience stress-related physical problems use the space below to describe them and how they affect your life.

_____

_____

_____

_____

_____

_____

_____

_____

_____

_____

_____

Parts Two and Three will give you strategies to help you overcome physical problems with stress.

Health anxiety (hypochondriasis)

Health anxiety is a stress-related problem where the focus of worry is physical symptoms. Sometimes this reflects an exaggerated concern about a genuine physical problem, sometimes the concern is about a problem for which there seems to be no evidence, sometimes health anxiety reflects the catastrophic prediction of ill health. Those with health anxiety are often extra-sensitive to normal physical sensations and/or preoccupied with the fear of catching a serious disease.

How health anxiety is maintained

Although sufferers seek repeated reassurances that they are well, they tend not to believe the advice they hear, or at least not for long. Constantly seeking reassurance isn't helpful because it prevents the sufferer from learning to assure him/herself and, thereby, overcome the health fears.

The problem is also maintained by repeated checking. This might be for signs of illness. We all have physical discomforts which are not serious and we all have occasional swellings and skin blemishes. Therefore, anyone who looks for these will find them and can be alarmed by the discovery. If a person goes on to prod and rub swellings or spots, they get worse and serve to frighten that person even more. Sufferers might also check out information about a physical problem, using books and the internet. This often provides information which fuels health-related worries.

Read Margaret's story below and underline anything you relate to.

CASE STUDY: Margaret

'I have always been concerned about my health, but I was never really worried until a year ago when I heard that awful story about the young mother who suddenly died of leukaemia, leaving three small children. I've got three children so the story really hit home and that day I began checking for swellings and bruises. I was soon carrying out a full body check three times a day and calling in to see my doctor every few days. He kept telling me that there was nothing to worry about and that I had probably caused small bruises by prodding my body so much. I'd feel OK for a while but my doubts always returned and my fears became stronger.

'Now, I also get my husband to check my body morning and evening so that I can feel confident that I haven't missed anything. He's getting fed up with this and we row a lot and this just makes me worse. Recently, my doctor has told me that he doesn't want to have to see me nearly every day at the surgery and I am finding it so hard not to go –

sometimes I pretend that one of the children is sick and use that as an excuse to get an appointment. The strange thing is, the more checking I do, the more worried I get but, as I see it, you can never be sure, can you?'

If you have health anxieties, use the space below to describe them and how they affect your life.

_____

_____

_____

_____

_____

_____

_____

_____

_____

_____

_____

_____

Parts Two and Three will give you strategies to help you overcome health anxiety.

Post-traumatic stress disorder (PTSD)

PTSD is a stress reaction which follows a traumatic event such as a road traffic accident, rape, or being witness to a major disaster. If you are suffering from PTSD along with the usual symptoms of anxiety, you will also usually experience recurring, vivid memories (flashbacks) or dreams of the event. Sometimes these are associated with intense emotions, such as tearfulness or terror. Sometimes the opposite occurs, and a person feels emotionally numb. Post-traumatic distress often follows a natural process of recovery that can take a few months to resolve, but sometimes it persists.

How PTSD is maintained

Although, for many people the stress associated with a trauma disappears over time, PTSD can become a long-term problem if a person avoids people, places or thoughts that stimulate memories of the event. By doing this, the memory continues to encapsulate a high level of fear which is not addressed. Although distressing, facing the memories of the trauma seems to be one of the most effective ways of dealing with PTSD.

Read David's story below and underline anything you relate to.

CASE STUDY: David

'After the car crash, I started to have dreams about it. I expected these to go away within a few days, but they were persistent and so vivid that I would wake up really believing that I had just relived the accident. My terrifying dreams continued for weeks and weeks and they were affecting my sleep and my ability to work the next day. Eventually, the doctor gave me some sleeping tablets to help me cope with this.

'Although I was then less bothered by the dreams I still could not bring myself to go back to the junction where the accident had happened, nor could I bring myself to drive the car again. I thought that I'd soon get over my fear of driving and of that junction, but I found that it got worse rather than better and I became very dependent on my wife to do the driving and to plan routes which didn't take in that junction. If we did get close to the scene of the accident, I would start to have really vivid memories – like a flashback of the original scene. This upset me so much that my wife soon learnt lots of alternative routes and we now stick to them. She's been so understanding about this and she has really put herself out to help. Although it's now been six months since the crash, I still don't feel confident that I will be able to drive again and being so restricted in my freedom to travel is affecting my work.'

If you have experienced PTSD, use the space below to describe your experience and how it affected your life.

_____

_____

_____

_____

_____

_____

_____

_____

_____

_____

Parts Two and Three will give you strategies to help you overcome PTSD.

Summary

1 Professionals use labels to classify and describe anxiety disorders and guide their choice of treatment: you might find it helpful to relate your difficulties to one or more of these categories.

2 You may be suffering from a combination of disorders, especially since they are often linked.

3 Whatever the label given to your anxiety problem, you can learn coping strategies that offer relief. These techniques are described in detail in Parts Two and Three.